Borders' Brick & Stone

The Eildon Hills from Standing Stone above Scott's View

Borders' Brick & Stone
A Journey in Pictures

By Bill and Isabel Kennedy

© Bill and Isabel Kennedy

First published in 1997
by The Pentland Press Limited
1 Hutton Close
Bishop Auckland
Durham

All rights reserved.
Unauthorised duplication contravenes existing laws.

ISBN : 1 85821 459 9

Printed and bound by
Lintons Printers, Crook, County Durham.

Dedicated to the memory of ISABEL KENNEDY

Foreword

The Borders - An area of great natural beauty; of rolling hills and gentle mountains, great rivers and rushing waterfalls; of agriculture and high technology, forestry and fish farms; of artists and poets, artisans and craftsmen; of hunting and shooting, rugby and salmon fishing; of historic battles and ancient legends, natural tragedies and heroic achievements; of great abbeys and castles, towers and fortified houses - The list is endless.

Happy accident led Isabel and myself to settle here. We 'discovered' the region during a holiday in 1988 and fell in love with it at first sight. With retirement due and our family scattered there was little to hold us in the Midlands, where we had spent the last six and a half years of my working life, or to pull us back to Glasgow, the city of our birth. A second visit convinced us to sell up and move.

As we drove down the main street into Melrose, the Rugby Club on the left, the market Square ahead and the peaks of the Eildons beyond, we both experienced an astonishing sensation of 'coming home' and our minds were made up. In May of the following year we set up home in the new town of Tweedbank, halfway between Melrose and Galashiels.

During the following four or five years we have increased our knowledge and appreciation of the area and the free time available to us in retirement has encouraged us to seek to set down our own, particular impressions of the Borders. As keen amateur photographers it seemed to us that the best way to do this would be in the form of a pictorial record and this book is the result.

We have chosen to concentrate on one aspect of the Borders' Scene, one which, as much as any other, can be said to have given it its character and individuality. The great Abbeys are rightly famous but there are so many other examples of the Stonemason's and Master Builder's craft which have much to tell us. Our lack of architectural expertise did not inhibit us as we were concerned more with the ambience and visual effect that each had created for us, as well as with the subject's pictorial quality - shape, colour and texture within the landscape. Only a limited selection could be included, of course, but we hope that the ones we have pictured may provide the stimulus to encourage you to explore the area and find favourites of your own.

We invite you to join us on a pilgrimage, albeit very different from the pilgrimage of the Northumbrian Monks who first came to this area many centuries ago. Our journey will lead you around an area bounded in the North and East by Berwick-on-Tweed and St Abbs and in the South and West by Langholm, Moffat and Peebles. You will not be faced by traffic jams in your car but will need to exercise caution during our many detours along narrow, winding roads. Waterproof Clothing and a sensible pair of walking shoes or boots could be useful for excursions on foot and you may also wish to carry your camera.

There is much to see............

Index

Chapter		Page
1.	Berwick on Tweed and Around	1
2.	Coldstream	5
3.	Around Duns	9
4.	The Coastal Strip	13
5.	Castles and Towers around Kelso	19
6.	Melrose v Galashiels	28
7.	Heading West	40
8.	The Scenic Route	45
9.	Through Eskdale to Langholm	48
10.	Hawick, the Unlikely Queen of the Borders	52
11.	The Last Lap	57

1. Berwick on Tweed and Around

I should make clear from the start that our Borders journey is more of a meandering than a tour but I have tried to keep each section within the bounds of what could be encompassed in the course of one or two days. There will, however, be quite a bit of retracing of steps, (and wheels), and it is inevitable that more will be missed than included. Still, I hope that you will see enough to whet the appetite and encourage further explorations without any guidance.

The River Tweed forms the boundary between Scotland and England for part of its length so where better to start our journey than in the bustling, Border town of Berwick. To all intents and purposes Berwick is no different in character from the other larger Scottish towns of the region and one could be forgiven for thinking that it lay in Berwickshire but this would be incorrect.

This well-fortified Royal Burgh, of which much of the walls and ramparts remains but which has seen its impressively sited castle crumble with the development of the Railways, is part of Northumberland and England. It was not always so. In the fifteenth century it was one of the four Royal Burghs of Scotland but it was given over to the "Auld Enemy" as part of a settlement with Edward IV. Subsequent attempts to have it returned to its rightful place have all foundered.

The enigma does not end here. As well as being divorced from the County bearing its name, it boasts a soccer team, Berwick Rangers, which plays in the Scottish Football League and, even more surprisingly, it was, until fairly recently, the Headquarters of the King's Own Scottish Borderers, one of Scotland's most celebrated Army Regiments.

Most of the buildings of the old town have long since disappeared but, amongst those remaining is the Holy Trinity Church, built between 1648 and 1653 by John Young, a Master of the Masons' Company. The church lacks a tower and stands somewhat foursquare but we still found it an impressive structure, though rather difficult to photograph due to the tall trees and substantial wall surrounding it.

There is much more to see during an extended walk around the town.

Within easy reach of Berwick are several other points of interest on both sides of the Border and a few of these are mentioned below.

A short drive out of town on the A698 will bring you in a short space of time to a minor road off to Horncliffe and the Union Bridge. This was designed by Captain Sir Samuel Brown and opened as a toll bridge in 1820. Its main claim to fame is that it was the first suspension bridge in Britain to carry vehicular traffic and it may be significant that the toll house, now demolished, was erected on the English side of the border! Now much strengthened and modernised, it still carries traffic of modest scale, only one vehicle at a time being allowed on the bridge. What struck us most about the bridge was what a marvellous feat of engineering it must have represented at the time it was first built, bearing in mind the width of the Tweed at that point.

Leaving the bridge, return to the A698, detouring to the B6470 to reach Norham. This is the site of another splendid Borders bridge which replaced an earlier, wooden structure, built on the orders of James IV of Scotland. This nervous monarch was concerned that he might drown while fording the Tweed at this point and determined to have a bridge built to avoid any future danger to his person. The bridge carries the B6470 to Ladykirk. Not far from it are the remains of a fine castle.

Norham Castle is an impressive ruin, its lofty keep above steep banks and guarded on two sides by a ravine and an artificial moat. It started off in 1121 as a timber castle and the great stone edifice grew up some fifty years later. Even Bruce, at the height of his powers, found it difficult to conquer and it was not until 1328, fourteen years after Bannockburn and still besieging Norham, that he managed to achieve the treaty of peace with England for which he had been striving. Sir Walter Scott used Norham Castle at the start of his epic, "Marmion". Little of the history of the place concerned us when we visited it but we marvelled at the quality of the workmanship and the fine proportions of the building.

Another magnificent house which should not be missed is Paxton, situated at the junction of the B6460 and B6461. This was built in 1758 by Patrick Home of Billie, later the thirteenth Laird of Wedderburn. It is one of the finest Neo-Palladian Mansions in the whole of Britain, based on the symmetrical style favoured by the famous sixteenth century architect, Andrea Palladio. The architects were two of the Adams family, John and James and the principal rooms were later embellished by Robert Adam. In 1811 George Home, the eighteenth Laird, commissioned Robert Reid, an architect noted for his work in Edinburgh, to build a picture gallery and library for the house and it now boasts the largest private gallery in Scotland. Recently restored, it is now used by the National Gallery of Scotland to house some of our greatest artistic treasures. The house is situated in about 70 acres of attractive parkland and woodland with good paths down by the Tweed.

Paxton House was originally planned by the Laird to become the marital home of himself and his intended bride, Miss de Brandt, the daughter of Frederick the Great of Prussia. Unfortunately, the wedding did not take place and only the house and a pair of frail silk gloves, a token of love from his betrothed, remain to remind us of this romantic dream.

Holy Trinity Church, Berwick

Paxton House

2. Coldstream

From Norham continuation on the A698 leads to Coldstream, which makes a suitable centre from which to visit the surrounding area. Coldstream sits on the Tweed and the river, again, forms the boundary between Scotland and England. The bridge here is particularly attractive, built by John Smeaton and completed in 1766. Since then it has been strengthened and widened during the 1960s.

Over this bridge, for his first ever visit to England on 7th May 1787, came our national bard, Robert Burns and, to mark the occasion, the local Burns Club erected a commemorative plaque on the bridge in 1926. The inscription bears the words of a prayer said to have been offered up by Burns as he knelt on the bridge before crossing.

"O Scotia! my dear, my native soil
 For whom my warmest wish to Heaven is sent
 Long may thy hardy sons of rustic toil
 Be blest with health, and peace, and sweet content."

There is nothing on record to provide evidence that the same, praiseworthy sentiments were expressed by the poet towards the English citizens he was about to visit!

The Coldstream Guards, one of our most renowned regiments, received the freedom of the burgh in 1968 and, in recognition of this honour, gifted a stone to the town. This stands on the spot from which General Monck commenced his historic march to London some three hundred years before, a march culminating in the restoration of Charles II to the Throne. Off Market Street is the Coldstream Guards' Museum, which is well worth a visit.

Another monument of note is the tall column in the Main Street in honour of Charles Marjoribanks, the first Liberal M.P. for Berwickshire.

Two miles west of Coldstream, off the A697 is the Hirsel, home of the late Lord Home, the ex Prime Minister. The house, of Georgian and Victorian design, is not open to the public but the grounds are attractive and contain a nature trail and wild fowl sanctuary.

Venturing over the border, still on the A697, will enable you to experience some of the atmosphere of one of the less happy episodes in Scottish history at Flodden Field. The battle which took place on that tragic day in 1513 saw scenes of slaughter remembered in song and legend throughout Scotland but nowhere more actively than in the Borders. The bodies of the dead were piled up in heaps in nearby Branxholme Churchyard. The site is marked by a simple, granite cross. The beauty of the landscape and the simplicity of the memorial did not reduce the emotional effect that our first visit to the site had on us.

"Where shiver'd was fair Scotland's spear
And broken was her shield" (Sir Walter Scott)

Commemorative Stone and view of the bridge at Coldstream

The Hirsel, home of the late Lord Home, ex Prime Minister

3. Around Duns.

Leaving Coldstream head for Duns on the A6112. The name of the town derives from an old word for a hill fort and the original settlement was built on the slopes of Duns Law. The town is an attractive residential centre with many fine houses and gardens. Beside the Council Offices is the "Jim Clark Room", a tribute to the world champion racing driver of that name. Clark was born in Fife but came to nearby Chirnside at the age of six and is buried in the churchyard there. Duns is within easy reach of a number of points of interest, among which is Manderston House, a few miles distant off the A6105.

Manderston is regarded as probably the finest Edwardian mansion in Scotland and our own impressions are in full agreement with those of the experts on this point. Starting out as a square building when it was built in 1790 for the first owner, it was developed in stages between 1890 until 1901 when, under the direction of the architect John Kinross, who had been responsible for the restoration of Falkland Palace for the third Marquis of Bute, it was completely remodelled for Sir James Miller. Above the new, main entrance door is the family coat of arms with the motto : Omne Bonum Superne - "all good comes from above". The house boasts a magnificent staircase with silver-plated balustrade and cantilevered marble stairs as well as a series of rooms of great splendour, featuring fine examples of French and Italian plasterwork. In our considered opinion it should not be missed!

The outbuildings include stables and domestic quarters offering an insight into life as it was at the turn of the century. The grounds and gardens are splendid and include a lake and fine trails to provide sufficient interest to repay a visit in themselves, even without the delights of the house.

Further along the A6105, a diversion on the B6355 will bring you to the village of Chirnside. The church is well positioned, on a small rise, close to the main street. It possesses a fine gateway, a memorial to the Liberal politician, Charles Marjoribanks. A feature of the church, which particularly appealed to us both is the Norman Doorway with its decorative chevron in the arch above. In the churchyard stands a simple stone in memory of Jim Clark, the racing driver and his reputation attracts tourists to the village.

Also off the A 6105 is another interesting church at Edrom. The original Parish church was built here around eleven hundred and five and, together with the surrounding lands, later became the property of the monks of Coldingham Priory. All that remains of the original building is a fine chancel arch with a chevron feature above the doorway similar to that at Chirnside.

This embellishment is typical of the Norman craftmanship to be seen in churches of the surrounding area. The more modern church now serving the village makes a fine contrast to this reminder of an earlier age.

A little further on is a good example of a tithe barn at Foulden, simple in itself but a reminder of how farmers would have had to hand over a portion of the fruits of their labours to the ruling gentry, much as we hand over our 'Tithe' to the Inland Revenue each year. As with many of the more prestigious buildings we have pictured, we were attracted by the warm texture of the stone rubble used in its construction.

Manderston House

Edrom Church

4. *The Coastal Strip.*

Since leaving Berwick we have concentrated on inland locations but now we are heading again towards the sea. When you have reached our starting point, pick up the A1 North, forking right on the A1107 towards Eyemouth. All the locations we have covered in this chapter can be reached easily from here.

Eyemouth sits at the point where the River Eye flows into the sea and the town grew up round its picturesque fishing harbour. It flourished as a fishing port as far back as the late sixteenth century, when the monks from nearby Coldingham Priory were the first to exploit its potential. Fishing is still a major activity though on a much reduced scale to that which it enjoyed in its heyday.

The perils of the sea were nowhere more evident than in this tiny fishing community in the October of eighteen eighty-one, when only a few of the thirty ships sailing out of the harbour returned safely. A sudden storm caused havoc with the fleet and one hundred and ninety-one men drowned, the bulk of them from Eyemouth.

This tragic event is commemorated by a museum which was set up in 1981 in the former "Auld Kirk". This includes a fifteen foot long tapestry sewn by local women, graphically telling the story of the disaster. The museum combines both the sights and sounds of the event and it provides quite an emotional experience.

Eyemouth is one of our favourite places to take visiting friends or relations and, on the first occasion when I went with my son, Graham, he stood on the golf course on the top of the cliffs, gazing down at the sea and the harbour and exclaimed :- "I must be in Heaven........and a golf course too!" I should say that, when we played round the course, the nearness of some of the fairways to the cliff edge and the strong breeze made sure that several stray "Dunlop 65s" ended up in the ocean for the Angels to pick up!

Before heading farther along the coastline and to provide a break from the sea air, a visit to Ayton Castle is well worth while. The B6355 leads directly to it from Eyemouth - a distance of about three miles.

The castle is an imposing, red sandstone building, designed by James Gillespie Graham, who was also responsible for Brodick Castle in the Isle of Arran. It was built for William Mitchell-Innes, then the Governor of the Bank of Scotland and has been a family home ever since, apart for a period during the Second World War, when it was used as a school. During the summer months the house is open to viewing on Wednesdays and Sundays and spectacular among its attractive features are the fine painted ceilings and Victorian furniture. The building is attractively situated, not on the rugged terrain associated with castles built to withstand the Border raids but in a setting consistent with a fine family home.

From here rejoin the A1107 and travel towards Coldingham. The town is quite secluded from the main road and has a less exhilirating atmosphere about it than we found at Eyemouth but it has a fine stretch of sand in its bay - ideal for family holidays - and this impression is backed up by its large caravan site.

The town was at one time an important religious centre, with a Benedictine priory dedicated to St Cuthbert founded in 1098 by Edgar, King of Scots. It is one of the oldest establishments of its kind in Scotland. The original priory was almost completely destroyed in repeated attacks and only a portion of the ruins survives. A new church was built around 1220 AD in the choir of the original building. This, too, suffered damage, notably at the hands of Cromwell in 1648 and the priory was completely renovated in 1954. Worship still takes place here.

Story has it that the great bell was removed from the original priory as the spoils of war and that it still sounds to this day in Lincoln.

A little farther along the coast is one of our favourite spots - St Abbs. The village is reached by a narrow and steep road and is much favoured by skin divers. The harbour is much tinier than that at Eyemouth but just as colourful. Attractive as it is, what brings us back regularly to the area is the cliff top walk from the nearby visitors' centre to the lighthouse and beyond. On a fine day, the views from the clifftop path are spectacular and the colonies of birds equally so. Recognition of the various species to be found is aided by visiting the audio/visual display at the centre prior to commencing the walk.

The walk at St Abbs is only moderately strenuous but, a few miles West of here, on an almost inaccessible stack, stands the remarkable ruin of Fast Castle. Meikle Black Law is the starting point for a walk to the castle but this should only be attempted by the fit and certainly not by any vertigo sufferer. The castle may be viewed from above but, even to approach this near, requires considerable effort.

Sir Walter Scott used Fast Castle as the model for his "Wolf's Crag" in the Bride of Lammermuir and wrote of it :-

"Imagination can scarce form a scene more striking, yet more appalling, than this rugged and ruinous stronghold, situated on an abrupt and inaccessible precipice, overhanging the raging ocean........."

This paints a much more vivid picture of the place than does our photograph, taken on a peaceful summer's day.

Having absorbed the atmosphere of this spectacular ruin, our next location will offer another and contrasting historical sample. We have farther to travel this time but there may well be points of interest jumping out at you, which priorities of space have forced us to exclude.

The A1107 leads us northwards to Cockburnspath, where the A1 South is followed to the village of Grantshouse. Here a series of minor roads leads the few miles to Abbey St Bathans and, again, put on your walking boots. The village is in the valley of the Whiteadder Water and a circular walk from here provides an abundance of variety; rippling streams and vigorous rapids, forests and heathland, Flora and Fauna - including white peacocks and rather aggressive geese!

The track leads you up the north-east slopes of Cockburn Law and here are situated the remains of the fortified hill fort of Edin's Broch. The Broch is open to view throughout the year and is one of only a few in Lowland Scotland, these constructions being much more common in the Highlands and Islands. It measures 90 feet in diameter and the walls, which contain small rooms or cells, are 9 feet thick in places. The main structure seems to have been an inner stronghold within a larger, oval fort, surrounded by earth ramparts. It is thought that it would have been occupied for a relatively short period of time - most probably during the first and second centuries.

Among the trees in the valley below sits the replacement for an ancient, Cistercian Priory. The original priory was created in the twelfth century but the Border Raids four hundred years later so damaged the building that only the east gable now remains and this is incorporated into the present church.

We have been over this walk on a number of occasions and manage to find new points of interest each time. Another advantage is that, at the end, the little restaurant at Abbey St Bathans will very pleasantly satisfy the appetite you have built up and prepare you for your next journey.

Ayton Castle

Eyemouth Harbour

Leaderfoot Viaduct, Gattonside

The Light and Fog Horn on the cliffs at St. Abbs

Fast Castle

5. Castles and Towers around Kelso

When we first experienced Kelso our immediate impression was how Continental it looked, particularly the design of the cobbled Main Square with its Town Hall. In character it seemed to us not dissimilar to Peebles, another town that we have yet to cover. Both appear, on the surface at least, to be more modern and less typical of a Borders' town yet, evidence of the old traditions still abound. Inhabitants of some of the other towns, for instance, might consider Kelso folk as being a bit 'uppish' although this scandalous allegation has never been proved to us.

To get to Kelso from where I left you at the end of the last chapter requires quite a bit of the 're-tracing of steps' I hinted at earlier but, since there is a spider's web of minor and major roads throughout the area, any of which will prove suitable, I leave the route to you. Having got there, however, I suggest you look first at the square and make up your own mind about what the town is saying to you.

Kelso is situated at a bend in the Tweed, where it is joined by its tributary, the Teviot, and entering it over Rennie's fine bridge leads directly past the remains of the abbey to the square. The original bridge collapsed in 1797 during a flood and, in recent years the replacement bridge, which is of limited width, was the scene of yet another catastrophe, when a fire engine attempting to avoid another vehicle drove through the parapet and crashed on to the bed of the river. One fireman lost his life but the results could have been even worse had the River Tweed been in spate at the time.

Kelso Abbey is thought to have been the wealthiest and most impressive of the Borders churches but only one small segment remains, towering over the roadway and fronted by attractive flower beds in the summer months. It was founded by David I and was settled by monks from the Picardy region of France, who had been at Selkirk from 1113. The abbey was garrisoned as a fortress during the campaigns of the Earl of Hertford in 1545, at which time the monks were killed and the huge structure reduced to its present state. The Norman influence on the architectural style is evident in the remaining west end of what was, at one time, a 300 feet long structure. During the eighteenth century the abbey was used for a time as the parish church but when, in accordance with the prediction of Thomas the Rhymer, the roof collapsed in 1771, worship here was abandoned for good.

In 1933 the widow of the eighth Duke of Roxburgh erected a memorial cloister to his memory. This was in a modern version of the abbey's Norman style and incorporated a doorway from the original cloister. The architect, Reginald Fairlie, also designed the main gateway to Floors Castle. Despite its warm and unweathered masonry, it is a graceful adjunct to its venerable companion.

Two very different castles may be viewed by driving to the edge of town on the A699 and following a marked path, on foot, along the Tweed. The first of these is Roxburgh Castle and, by climbing up among its ruins, the second, Floors, comes into sight on the plain in the distance.

Only a few humps remain of Roxburgh Castle to hint at the mighty fortress which stood on this imposing site so many centuries ago. Here it was that Bruce's sister, Mary, was hung in a cage from 1306 until 1310 and here also James II of Scotland was killed by an exploding cannon, similar to 'Mons Meg'.

If Roxburgh was designed and located as a stronghold to repulse a determined enemy, Floors is a castle of a different complexion. Its situation offers no difficulties of approach and its construction is unashamedly decorative. Designed originally in 1721 by William Adam, it was much extended some hundred and twenty years later by Playfair, whose imagination provided it with its present exotic outline.

It boasts of having one window for each day of the year and contains fine collections of porcelain, tapestries and French furniture. Its art collection includes examples by Canaletto, Gainsborough, Rayburn and Reynolds. The whole provides a magnificent family home for its present owner, the Duke of Roxburgh, Chief of the Ker Clan, and his Duchess.

To view the castle and its gardens, very worthwhile, means a short drive on the marked route from Kelso town centre.

Leaving Kelso behind, take the A6089 towards Gordon, diverting on the minor road to Mellerstain House. This elegant Georgian mansion was built in 1720 for the Baillie family by William and Robert Adam and it is now the home of the Earl and Countess of Haddington. The magnificent Adam ceilings are alone worth a visit but the house also contains a superb selection of paintings, including works by Van Dyk, Constable and Gainsborough. The gardens were laid out in 1909 by Sir Reginald Blomfield and include many fine trees, avenues and a lake.

Back on the A6089, a mile or two further on you will reach Gordon and, here, turn left on to the A6105. On your right, on the edge of the town is the Greenknowe Tower. The tower was built in 1581 on the site of an earlier building founded by the knight, Aidan of Gordun. From him the line of succession passed through the Setons - whose coat of arms is carved over the door of the tower - to the Pringles of Stichel. When a fairly low sun plays on the building, it brings out the warmth of the stonework most effectively.

Rejoin the A6089 and continue until it merges with the A697 towards Lauder. Just outside the town is Thirlestane Castle, one of the oldest castles in Scotland.

Built originally in the thirteenth century as a defensive fort, it was rebuilt and enlarged three centuries later and became the home of the Maitlands, Earls of Lauderdale. The castle has been further enlarged and embellished over the years but remains home to the Maitland family to this day. Built of local, warm red rubble, it rises to three storeys and an attic. Like many of the fine Borders houses it possesses magnificently furnished state rooms and fine plasterwork ceilings but we found particularly intriguing the family nursery, with its large collection of historic toys.

From Lauder travel south on the A68 towards Earlston. Here, head east on the A6105 for a short distance, then fork right on the B6397 towards Smailholm. A minor road takes you to Smailholm Tower. This famous Borders landmark moved Sir Walter Scott to pen the following lines :-

> *"These crags, that mountain tower*
> *Which charmed my fancy's waking hour*
> *Methought grim features, seamed with scars,*
> *Glared through the windows' rusty bars."*

The tower sits on the summit of a rocky hill, close by the farm of Sandyknowe, where Scott spent much of his childhood. Rubble-built again, with facings of red sandstone, it rises to four storeys and has an oblong plan. One unusual feature is a projecting dormer window above the entrance to the south wall.

In the sixteenth century, from when it is believed to date, it would have been enclosed by a barmekin or curtain wall and courtyard and the remains of other buildings are still visible to the west. The whole was known as a Peel or Pale and this is the source of the term 'Peel Tower'. An excellent historical exhibition is on display inside and, climbing the steps to the top of the fifty-seven foot tower leads to a parapet walk offering spectacular views.

Continuation on the B6397 will bring you back to Kelso or, if you wish to go directly to our next centre, a double header, turning sharp right before Kelso on the B6404 will lead through St Boswells and, via the A68, to Melrose/Galashiels.

Kelso Town Square

Floors Castle, home of the Duke of Roxburgh

Mellerstain House

Thirlestane Castle, near Lauder

Smailholm Tower

Borders' Brick & Stone

Memorial Cloister at Kelso Abbey

The Greenknowe Tower

6. Melrose v Galashiels.

To mention Galashiels and Melrose in the same sentence is to take a risk. The two towns are rivals in a great many ways, not least in the sporting scene, where they challenge one another for leadership of the Scottish and Borders Rugby Union leagues. However, they are only a few miles apart and share proximity with several points of interest ; besides, we live in the middle, at Tweedbank, and split our loyalties between the two. A toss of the coin has decided that Galashiels should be first to be dealt with so here goes.

The town is second only to Hawick in terms of population and grew up around a thriving woollen industry, now reduced to a fraction of its original importance. The Valley Mill behind Market Street remains and organised tours here allow visitors to learn of the major part played by wool in the town's development and, of course, to purchase items in the Mill Shop. The Scottish College of Textiles nearby is regarded as one of the most advanced establishments of its kind and is a mecca for aspiring textile leaders.

There are many buildings of historic interest and Old Gala House, formerly the seat of the Pringles, is one of the most prominent examples. The house is much changed from its original state and now acts as a community and arts centre. It is built of small local rubble throughout.

One building depicted is the clock tower of the Municipal Buildings designed by Sir Robert Lorimer and, in front of it, the fine war memorial in the form of the bronze Border Reivers' Statue by Thomas Clapperton. This stands at the head of Bank Street, the main thoroughfare, flanked on one side by attractive gardens, which have replaced the mill buildings and cottages that once stood there.

All that remains of the old Parish Church of the burgh is Gala Aisle, which stands in the ancient churchyard. The climax of the "Braw Lads Gathering" - Galashiels' own annual Rideout and commemoration of Borders' legend - is a church service in the grounds of this, one of the oldest buildings in the town.

Moving on to Melrose, one feature that cannot fail to capture the imagination is its magnificent setting beneath the Eildon Hills.

> *"O Eildon Hills, huge sisters three,*
> *As fair you rise as ony,*
> *Scotia has higher hills than thee*
> *But few gleam half as bonny."*

These words of the eighteenth century poet, Andrew Scott of Bowden could not be bettered. The hills, of volcanic origin, have played their part in determining with their red soil the character of many of the rubble-built buildings of the surrounding area. The three peaks give rise to the name "Trimontium" for the Roman camp which existed at their base and a Trimontium Museum is featured in the town centre.

In summer there is a constant flow of tour buses carrying visitors to the abbey, Abbotsford House and the other nearby attractions. The abbey was founded by Cistercian Monks in 1136 and one of its first Abbots was St Cuthbert. Lying on the Middle March, close to the old Roman route from Corbridge to the Lothians, it was at the mercy of any raiding force, leading to frequent pillaging and burning. One such act of destruction was during the 'Rough Wooing' of Henry VIII in his attempts to have the young Mary Queen of Scots handed over as bride for the then Prince of Wales, later Edward VI.

The building of mellow, rose red sandstone is a magnificent ruin and has been enjoyed by us both on many occasions. One particularly intriguing visit was on the last evening of the Melrose annual celebrations, when we attended the final ceremony in the abbey. The low evening light added a particular magic to the scene.

There are a number of fine examples of carvings to have survived and one of these and its associated legend intrigued us. This is a figure of the Virgin Mary carrying the child, Jesus. The head of the baby is missing and the story goes that, in the course of attempted desecration by a workman during the Reformation, the head fell from the statue on to him, crippling him for life.

Robert the Bruce is one of many notable figures associated with the abbey. On his deathbed he instructed his good companion, Sir James Douglas to cut out his heart after his death and carry it with him against the "Infidel" before burying it in Melrose Abbey. Douglas was slain but the casket containing the heart, after lengthy travels round Europe, is said to have found its final resting place under the Chancel's East window. Other famous families who have been buried within the abbey include members of the Scotts, Pringles and Douglases.

The abbey is now in the care of the Secretary of State for Scotland and is open to visitors all the year round.

A short distance from Melrose, on the banks of the Tweed and near to the new town of Tweedbank, stands Abbotsford House, the home of Sir Walter Scott from 1811 until his death in 1832. Scott was determined to create the finest possible house to complement its wonderful location and bankrupted himself in the attempt. It remains a lasting monument to the man and his works.

Before he bought and improved the property it was known as "Clarty Hole" - a dirty place - but Scott had the old house demolished and replaced it with the splendid edifice we can now visit. It is regarded by the experts as something of a hotch potch in design - sham Gothic combined with a Baronial style and featuring slim turrets and oriel windows - but it remains, for us, a magnificent structure and, viewed from across the River Tweed, presents an impressive picture.

Across the River Tweed from Melrose is the village of Gattonside. A drive through here and past the old railway viaduct at Leaderfoot leads by way of a minor road on the right to the famous viewpoint known as "Scott's View". This was a favourite spot for Scott and story has it that, while his horses were drawing his funeral carriage from Abbotsford to his last resting place in Dryburgh Abbey, the horses automatically paused at that point. A commemorative stone stands at the spot, one from which more paintings and photographs will have been created than, perhaps, at any other location in the Borders. A slightly different prospect of the same view may be obtained by climbing the hill on the opposite side of the road to a standing stone. Fine views from this spot are available in all directions.

Continuing on the same road past the viewpoint and down the hill will bring you to another well known house at Bemersyde. For eight hundred years Bemersyde has been in the possession of the Haig family and the present owner is the thirtieth Laird. Thomas the Rhymer prophesied as follows :-

*"Tyde what may, what e'er betyde,
Haig shall be Haig of Bemersyde"*

The peel tower which forms the central part of the house was built in 1535 and two wings were added in 1795 and 1859 respectively. The gardens in their present form were designed and laid out by Field Marshall Earl Haig, the twenty-ninth Laird, and are open to the public throughout the summer, along with attractive riverside walks.

A short distance on leads to a small lay-by with a path off to a statue of William Wallace. On the first occasion that we visited this we were doubly astonished - firstly by the sheer size of the figure but also by the fact that it had been erected in such a location. Until relatively recently it had been almost inaccessible but there is now a clear path through the trees and shrubbery leading directly to the statue and the large stone urn beside it.

The sculpture was carried out in 1814 to the instruction of David Stuart Erskine, Earl of Buchan. He was of the opinion that Wallace had received less than his fair share of fame relative to Bruce and was determined to put this right. He certainly did so in style!

The statue itself is enormously impressive but, even more so, is the prospect offered to its unseeing eyes of the land Wallace had strived so hard to wrest from the English yoke. In our opinion the best view to be obtained is from the field behind, even though this limits the detail which can be recorded in the statue. One intriguing, if unlikely, story we heard recently is that, some sixty years ago, an American tourist broke off the little finger of the statue's left hand, (Even after his death Wallace had to suffer), and took it home as a souvenir. The hand has, indeed, been repaired, probably during the complete restoration of the statue financed by a local appeal set up by the Saltire Society in 1991. The inscription at the base shows the following :-

"Erected by David Stuart Erskine, Earl of Buchan.
WALLACE
GREAT PATRIOT HERO! ILL REQUITED CHIEF
Joannes Smith, Sculpsil - **A.D.MDCXIV"**

John Smith was a local man from the attractive village of Darnick on the outskirts of Melrose.

The large urn on the opposite side of the path from the statue is inscribed with a eulogy to William Wallace, parts of which have worn away with the passage of time but enough remains to confirm both the high regard in which Wallace was held by the writer and also the hatred felt by most Scots towards Edward, the English King.

Having retraced your steps, continue down the road and turn right at a junction towards Dryburgh Abbey.

The abbey is built of local, pinky-grey stone, which is less red than Melrose but glows warmly when the light is favourable. It was founded by Hugh de Morville, a Norman Baron who, with the assistance of David I, brought monks from Alnwick in Northumberland to the banks of the Tweed in the twelfth century. Like all of the Borders abbeys, Dryburgh suffered devastation on numerous occasions and, following its sacking by the Earl of Hertford in 1544, it was never rebuilt.

Parts of the church are still well preserved, including the chapel adjoining the North Transept in which are buried the remains of Sir Walter Scott. Field-Marshall Earl Haig, Commander of the British forces in the First World War is also buried close by. Only the Scotts of Abbotsford, the Haigs of Bemersyde and the Erskines, Earls of Buchan are entitled to be buried in the abbey.

To us Dryburgh Abbey seems to have an air of tranquility and it is very easy to wander around the grounds and among the ruins with no awareness of the passing of time. In the grounds stands an unusual sculpture, depicting on one side James I and on the other James II. The significance of this escaped us but we have heard that the work was carried out by a local stone mason, perhaps also the creator of the Wallace statue. We have been unable to verify this.

In the same general area are several other points of interest, including the Dryburgh Abbey Hotel and the imposing Mertoun House and Gardens. After visiting the hotel, turn right at the end of the road and, some distance on, right again on to the road to St Boswells. Cross the Mertoun Bridge and the entrance to Mertoun House is on the left.

The house was designed by Sir William Bruce for William Scott of Harden and built between 1703 and 1705 to replace a former mansion house. There are a number of specimen trees in the grounds, likely to have been planted before the existing house was built and, also of interest, is a well preserved circular dovecot dated 1567, thought to be the oldest in the country. The house is the home of the Duke of Sutherland but only the grounds and gardens are open to the public.

Our visit to Mertoun towards the end of our project was one of our most rewarding days but we were quite unprepared for its magnificence. Externally, the house compares very favourably with, for example, Manderston or Paxton, both of which enjoy much greater publicity and, in addition, the gardens are among the finest that we have come across. I have no doubt that we will visit it many times.

Back in Melrose, a short distance up the B6359 leads to the village of Bowden. A pleasant village with a green, it is graced with a fine church, situated on a bank above a tree-shaded burn. This church was founded in 1128 by monks from Kelso but was practically rebuilt in 1644 and again restored in 1909 to its present condition . The interior is simple and tranquil, making a peaceful spot on a warm summer's day to cool down before moving on to our next destination - a very different kind of Borders town but with plenty of charm of its own.

Melrose Abbey

Melrose Abbey Museum

Abbotsford House, home of Sir Walter Scott

Bemersyde House, home of the Haig Family for centuries

The Wallace Statue

Bowhill House

Mertoun House

A Dovecote in the grounds of Mertoun House

Dryburgh Abbey

Galashiels Municipal Buildings

7. Heading West

The A 72 west of Galashiels passes through Clovenfords.   Here is one of the many statues of Sir Walter Scott to be found in the area. This one is neither the most attractively located nor, in our opinion, particularly memorable but it is prominent in our minds for its capacity to change colour.   When we saw it first it was dirty grey and flaking.   A year or two later it had been painted - wait for it - lilac!   This did not last - public pressure brought an early rethink and it is, once again, a neutral greyish colour.

Driving on we pass through Walkerburn, with its Scottish Textiles Museum, and on to Innerleithen and St Ronan's Wells. Centuries ago the well above the village was regarded as 'Holy' and there is said to have been a priory or kirk there at that time, in charge of the monk, Ronan.   The famous spa of St Ronan's Wells owes its name to him.

Bottled water may still be obtained from the friendly caretakers although the site now also serves as a fitness centre, opened by Yvonne Murray, the athlete, some years back.   Behind the buildings an attractive garden, including a formal arrangement of healing herbs, leads up to the well itself and a tap in the caretaker's office provides samples for tasting.   It must be good for you.......!

At Innerleithen a left turn on to the B709 brings you to Traquair in about a mile.   The house is said to be the oldest inhabited house in Scotland, owned by the Maxwell Stuarts and open to the public daily from May to September.

The origins are obscure, although the brochure speaks of Alexander I having signed a charter here over 800 years ago, but what is certain is that the property was much altered through the sixteenth and seventeenth centuries.

The existing building is 120 feet in length, rises to four storeys and a garrett and the walls are roughcasted and painted.   There are a number of fine rooms and, in one of these, Mary Queen of Scots lodged with Darnley in 1566.   'Queen Mary's Room' is little changed from its original state.

A set of gates at the end of a long avenue from the house are known as the 'Bear Gates' due to the decorative stonework. These gates are said to have remained closed since Bonny Prince Charlie passed through them in 1745.   The Jacobite history of the house supports one of many explanations put forward for the permanent closure of this entrance - that they will not be reopened 'until the Stuarts are restored to the throne of Britain' - unlikely now!

A number of festivals take place in the grounds during the year and these also accommodate an active crafts community. Traquair Ale continues to be brewed for sale on the premises.

Yet a few more miles along the A72 and the Royal Burgh of Peebles comes into view. To us, neither the burgh nor its inhabitants quite fits the pattern for Borders towns but it is, undoubtedly, an extremely smart and attractive place to visit for all that. One theory for the differences was offered to us by an inhabitant of Innerleithen. Her view was that, whereas in Innerleithen, Selkirk, Jedburgh and so on the population, by and large, lived and worked in their locality, a high percentage of Peebles residents emanated from and commuted to Edinburgh to work. As Glaswegians, we knew exactly what she meant but we had better not elaborate!

Through the town runs a fine, broad street flanked by a number of imposing buildings as well as the main shops. One building which we particularly like is the Chambers Institution, part of which dates from the fifteenth century. This is now used as a civic centre and also contains a fascinating museum. The name derives from William Chambers of encyclopaedia fame, who gifted the building to the town.

The River Tweed runs alongside the town and, at the west end, is crossed by a fine bridge. This bridge, or the carpark beside it, is the starting point for one of our favourite walks. This leads through a large area of parkland and follows a track along the river. The walk is elastic and can extend to a three and a half hour round trip, passing the old railway bridge and on along the disused line etc, or may be a relatively short stroll to Neidpath Castle and back.

Neidpath Castle is superbly situated on a high bluff above the river. Built in the fourteenth century, it has since been remodelled several times, principally in the seventeenth century. As well as being a fortress, it has served as a home for the Fraser and Hay families but is now in the care of the Wemyss and March Estates. They have carried out a programme of restoration with some assistance from the National Trust for Scotland. The tower is rubble-built and rises to five storeys and a garret, the masonry being as much as ten feet thick in places. It is open to the public and provides a magnificent prospect of the Tweed from its heights.

In 1897, to celebrate the Diamond Jubilee of Queen Victoria, Peebles inaugurated an annual festival known as the Beltane Festival. Though each of the Borders towns has a different basic theme for its own annual celebration, most of these include mass rideouts as an important element and Peebles is no exception. During their ceremonies, the chosen young man - the 'Cornet', as he is known, along with his 'Lass' and their supporters ride the marches and halt at Neidpath for a ceremony conducted by the 'Warden of Neidpath', a prominent local figure.

Returning from Neidpath along the main road to Peebles, there is a fine tower on the left. The original St Andrew's Tower was built in the twelfth century but this was destroyed in English raids four hundred years later. A fragment of the foundations remains and, attached to this, is a plaque. The tower was restored in 1858 and makes an imposing landmark on the edge of the town.

A view of the main street in Peebles

Neidpath Castle, Peebles

Statue of James Hogg, the Ettrick Shepherd

8. The Scenic Route

Our route out of Peebles is in a generally southerly direction with Moffat the suggested point at which to pause. Start off on the A72 west and take the B712 junction past Drumelzier until it meets the A701. The region through which you will be passing is one that we find particularly attractive and many photo opportunities present themselves. However, our brief means that we have concentrated our attention on 'Brick, Stone and Rock', although you may detect a certain increased flexibility in our interpretation of these subjects where we just 'couldn't resist'! If you drive the route, you may well understand why.

South on the A 701, just before Tweedsmuir is the famous old meeting place of the Covenanters, the Crook Inn. To be honest, although we were aware that the inn was one of the oldest in the Borders and that Robert Burns met there often with cronies of his, little of this illustrious past came through to us. The building has been much restored and modernised and, during these alterations, the character has, inevitably, changed. On the inside it was much more possible to visualise how it might have been, helped by the decor and memorabilia on display. These include a poster quoting from the Burns poem, 'Willie Wastle', which he is reputed to have composed in the old kitchen, now the bar.

A minor road to the left, a little way on from here, leads past the two picturesque reservoirs of Talla and Megget, both of which make splendid subjects for the camera. The road up to the reservoirs is narrow and winding and there are several steep climbs and descents but traffic is sparse and the views are spectacular.

The road is a delight to drive, as it continues to wind and, eventually, descend to meet the A 708 at St Mary's Loch. Our destination is at the head of the loch, where it joins its companion, the Loch of the Lowes and where, also, stands another fine old inn, Tibbie Shiels.

The inn stands in a marvellous setting on the shores of the loch, overlooked by a fine statue of the 'Ettrick Shepherd' - the poet James Hogg. He is said to have gathered here on many an occasion with his compatriots Thomas Carlyle, Walter Scott and Robert Louis Stevenson. Tibbie Shiels was very much a character in her own right and one can only imagine the content of the conversation that must have flowed in the back kitchen of her inn, when those famous literary figures got together over a dram or two. It remains a focal point for visitors to the area.

Continuing south along the A708 leads past the Grey Mare's Tail, a spectacular waterfall with opportunities for fine walks and a herd of mountain goats. This road brings you, at last, to Moffat, the far south-west point of the area we intended to cover.

Moffat is a pleasant town with a broad main street, some fine buildings and, probably its most famous landmark, the Ram Statue, a reminder of just how important sheep and the woollen industry has been to the whole of the Borders Region.

Talla Reservoir

Meggett Reservoir

9. Through Eskdale to Langholm

Our next destination leads to the southernmost point on our trail and, like the previous chapter, much of the beauty to be seen is in the drive itself. This provides some excuse for the extremely circuitous route we have set out.

Back we head on the A708 to St Mary's Loch and on until the junction with the B709, where we turn back on ourselves to return south. The route passes through a number of interesting locations of which we have picked out only one or two. One of these is Ettrick and nearby Ettrick Hall where James Hogg was born in 1770. At this point I will allow myself the luxury of a small digression

In our (less than perfect) attempts to convey our impressions of how stone and warm brick have contributed to the natural beauty of the Borders, it was inevitable that we should grow to appreciate, also, the debt we owe to others long since dead, in fields far beyond the scope of our brief. The beauties that we now enjoy are the legacy we have inherited from these generations, whose skill and often superhuman efforts during their lifetimes, achieved a perfection at which we can only marvel.

Unlike Burns and Scott, Hogg's worth as a lover of humanity and as a poet were slow to achieve recognition but the following short extract, which is just the thing for you to reflect on during your picnic beside the Ettrick Water, shows an insight as perceptive as that of any of his contemporaries.

> *How foolish are mankind to look for perfection*
>   *In any poor changeling under the sun!*
> *By nature, or habit, or want of reflection.*
>   *To vices and folly we heedlessly run.*
> *The man who is modest and kind in his nature,*
>   *And open and cheerful in every degree;*
> *Who feels for the woes of his own fellow-creature,*
>   *Though subject to failings, is dear unto me.*
>   (The Forest Minstrel)

If you've finished your lunch we can now move on and, for anyone unaware of its existence, our next location will come as a surprise. Close to Eskdalemuir is the Tibetan Temple of Samye-Ling. The Kagyu Samye-Ling Temple was inaugurated by Kentin Tai Situ-PA and David Steel, M.P. on 8th August 1988 and, although a long way short of being completed, its colourful carved and painted roof is very different from what one would expect to see in the valley of the River Esk.

Having put your shoes back on after leaving the temple, the drive continues along the B709 as far as Langholm.

The town is within a few miles of the border with England and we have passed through it countless times on our way north and south on the A7. Until recently we had driven through with no real awareness of what the town was like. In fact we found it to be one of the most attractive in the whole of the region, standing at the confluence of three rivers and with a number of fine and contrasting bridges. Calling itself the 'Muckle Toon', it actually grew from two separate villages, the 'old and new toons', which flourished on opposite banks of the Esk, each with its own character. It contains a number of interesting buildings.

Tibetan Temple of Samye-Ling

View of Langholm from the top of Whita Hill

10. Hawick, the Unlikely 'Queen of the Borders'

On the way to Hawick and a short distance from Langholm are memorials to two of that town's most prominent citizens, each of which is well worth seeing. Both are reachable from the same parking spot and provide an opportunity to stretch the legs.

Start off north on the A7 and, almost immediately on the right is a minor road off to Newcastleton. A short distance along this, on the right, is a track up the 1,162 feet high Whita Hill. The summit opens up fine views in all directions and, here too, stands a 100 feet Obelisk erected to the memory of General Sir John Malcolm.
Malcolm was born in 1769 and died in London in 1833, being buried in Westminster Abbey. He is remembered mainly for his work in India where he was the Governor of Bombay.

The other much more recent memorial is situated at the start of the walk up Whita Hill and is in honour of Christopher Murray Grieve, better known as Hugh MacDiarmid, who was born in Langholm in 1892 and died in 1978. This takes the unusual form of a bronze and steel sculpture shaped like an open book, depicting pictorial representations of the subjects most dear to the poet. The work was paid for by public subscription and unveiled in 1985. Its creator was Jake Harvey, a metal worker from Maxton. We found the sculpture intriguing but it is not universally popular.

This minor road over the hills will bring you to another, quite different town at Newcastleton. This little town was founded by the Duke of Buccleuch as a weaving centre in the late eighteenth century and it is laid out as a single long main street, interrupted at intervals by a series of formal squares. Our impression was of an 'old world' atmosphere and several of the shops contributed to this ambience with displays of antique and Edwardian goods. Everything about the town was extremely orderly and the more recent building work seemed to have been planned to maintain this feature.

Leaving Newcastleton, head north on the B6357 and, in a mile or so, take the left fork on the B6399 towards the Hermitage. This is situated off a minor road to the left.

If Floors is a castle in name only, The Hermitage represents the antithesis, a stronghold paying little court to ideas of charm or beauty. Founded in 1244, it ressembles a flattened cube, with few features on its exterior to relieve the feeling of grim solidity.

The stark and forbidding atmosphere we sensed when observing it is fully supported with what we have learned of its history. One of the Soulis Family, who originally occupied the castle, Lord William, was notorious for his cruelty. A favourite pastime of his was to invite noble neighbours to dine with him and take this opportunity to have them murdered. It was even alleged that he sold his soul to the devil and that his devilish master returns every seven years to open up the chamber beneath the ruins where the bargain was struck. Other legend has it that he was put to death, on the orders of the King, by being wrapped in sheet lead and boiled in a huge cauldron inside a Druid circle near the castle.

More likely to be authentic is the history that the Earl of Bothwell, while recuperating after injury at the castle, was visited by Mary Queen of Scots from where she was living at Jedburgh. Mary is said nearly to have died from the exertions of the long ride she undertook.

The castle has been used in a number of film settings, including 'Macbeth' and 'Mary Queen of Scots'.

The drive to Hawick from here, always on the B6399, is another scenic delight. The road is narrow and winding with passing points. As a result, constant care is necessary but the absence of many other vehicles and the views, at least for the passengers, are rewarding compensations. One particularly spectacular prospect we found included a fine railway viaduct to be seen close to the village of Shankend.

Hawick describes itself as the 'Queen of the Borders' but this seems, to us, a somewhat inapt description. Virility and an aggressive air of confidence are the qualities that spring to our minds when we think of Hawick, valuable attributes in themselves but scarcely what one would look for in a 'queen'. Perhaps the title of 'Queen' that it claims as its own relates purely to how it sees its place in the pecking order among the Tweed and Knitwear industries of the Borders.

Its setting is a fine one, in a green valley bisected by the Teviot and with good examples of the old mill buildings but, we have to confess, we feel more drawn by the grace of Kelso, the charm of Melrose or the friendliness of Galashiels. Nonetheless, Hawick contributes as much as any of the others I have mentioned to the 'whole picture' and, unlike Kelso, for all its charm, it seems a much more typical member of the Borders family.

The theme of the Hawick annual Common Riding celebrations speaks volumes for the town's character. A year after the tragedy of Flodden a group of English raiders, following drunken carousing after pillaging the village of Denholm, were massacred in their sleep by the young men from Hawick, said to have been the sons of the very men who had died the previous year at Flodden. Every year, Hawick commemorates this exploit. Somehow or other, we can visualise this happening but it is difficult to imagine young men from Kelso becoming involved in a similar escapade. "Thus respectability doth make cowards of us all"- as Shakespeare might have said, had he lived in Kelso.

William Beattie's fine statue of a horse and rider, erected in 1914 to commemorate the four hundredth anniversary of a successful skirmish against the English is pictured. Sadly, the sculptor was killed on active service during the Great War, which started soon after.

Shankend Railway Viaduct

Mill Building in Hawick

Elliott Memorial Statue, Hawick

11. The Last Lap

Our final journey will end up at the last of the great abbeys - Jedburgh - but before that we have a good number of miles to cover, with at least a few of these on foot.

The route is northwards on the A7 towards Selkirk, around which are several of the features we have chosen to illustrate. The town itself is well worth some of your time, with a number of interesting buildings, including Sir Walter Scott's old Courtroom, a restoration of one of the old mill buildings - part financed by the E.C. - and a statue erected in honour of Mungo Park, the explorer, who was killed in Africa at an early age. Thomas Clapperton added the decorative panels to Andrew Currie of Darnick's fine figure.

Selkirk has the largest 'Rideout' and, arguably, the most authentically founded annual celebration of the historic battles in the Borders. According to the story, only one man from the large number who left Selkirk to fight at Flodden came back alive. On reaching the town square, he is said to have produced a tattered banner rescued from the fray, lowered it and cast it in the dust as symbol of the disaster. This scene is re-enacted each year as part of the pageantry by a young man chosen from the community.

Four miles south-west of Selkirk is a fine Georgian house, Bowhill, owned by the Duke of Buccleuch. The house and grounds are open during the summer months and, frequently, it features entertainments or exhibitions of general interest in a small theatre. The house contains a superb collection of furniture, china and paintings, including a famous example of Sir Walter Scott painted by Raeburn. On show are a number of items belonging to Scott, including his manuscript of 'The Lay of the Last Minstrel', in which Bowhill featured :-

> *When summer smiled on sweet Bowhill,*
> *And July's eve, with balmy breath,*
> *Waved the bluebells on Newark-Heath;*
> *When throstles sung in Harehead shaw,*
> *And corn was green on Carterhaugh,*
> *And flourished, broad, Blackandro's oak*
> *The aged Harper's soul awoke!*

The grounds, too, are worth a visit and include a peaceful lake, beyond which the house presents itself to be pictured.

Just a little further along the same road, the A708, the tower of Newark Castle can be seen. This is in a strong position, crowning the right bank of the Yarrow and it boasts walls of up to ten feet in thickness. It has a bloody history.

At nearby Philiphaugh in 1645 took place one of the cruellest of the Borders' battles. Royalist forces, outnumbered ten to one by the Covenant army under General David Leslie were overwhelmingly defeated. All those captured, including non-combatants together with three hundred women and children, were murdered afterwards in the name of Religion. A hundred of these were put to death in the courtyard of the castle.

Back towards Selkirk and off it to the B7009 takes you to another of the many peel towers in the area - Aikwood Tower. This example is unusual as it has been completely restored to become the family home of Sir David Steel, M.P. In a converted byre building adjoining the tower, the Byres of Aikwood Trust, a registered charity, has established a permanent exhibition of the life and work of James Hogg, the Ettrick Shepherd. Sir David's wife, Judy, is administrator for the trust, which has a flexible approach to the housing of seminars; music, theatre and dance projects; even wedding ceremonies!

> *Sae Willie took Meg to the Forest sae fair*
> *And they lived a maist happy and peaceable life*
> *The langer he knew her; he lo'd her the mair*
> *For a prudent, a virtuous and sensible wife.*
> (From The Fray of Elibank - James Hogg)

It is, perhaps, time to ask you to stretch your legs again and what we have in mind should do this adequately. The walk starts from a small car park beside Philiphaugh Farm. To reach this, leave Selkirk by the bridge over the Ettrick Water, take the left fork where the road divides and, when you meet the main road, cross it directly and follow the metalled road beside the farm to the parking spot.

The track is waymarked, leading through conifer woods to a small reservoir, then upwards by a burn, curving to meet a forestry plantation to the north. It follows this for a time then leaves it for the last climb to the peak of the Three Brethren, named for its distinctive trio of cairns. The height is about 1500 feet and the views can justifiably be described as breathtaking. All of the Border hills are in evidence, most obviously the Eildons to the East.

The total distance of the round trip back to the car park will be in the region of eight miles so allow yourself plenty of time and carry something to drink if the weather is hot.

Before heading for Jedburgh and the end of our journey, a couple of miles along the A7 towards Galashiels will provide an opportunity to view the old Selkirk Brig, the route followed by traffic before the building of the by-pass. If you are lucky, there may be a fisherman in the middle of the river to make a photo opportunity even more attractive.

Back at Selkirk, follow the A699 as far as St Bothwells then the A68 south towards Jedburgh. Before then, however, we have one last detour for you to make. At the junction with the B6400, turn left towards the Harestanes Visitors' Centre. This makes a very interesting outing, particularly for children, and offers a number of walks of varying length. The longest of these - the Green Route - is the one we have in mind for you. This, like that to the Three Brethren, is in a generally upward direction but of a much more gentle nature. Your destination is the Wellington Monument on Peniel Heugh and a round trip should not take more than an hour and a half at the most.

The monument is in the form of a tower, 150 feet in height above the 740 feet high Peniel Heugh. Building of the tower commenced two weeks after Waterloo in 1815 but the wooden top was added in 1867. The work was commissioned by the 6th Marquis of Lothian and the present holder of the title has his home on the nearby estate at Monteviot House. This, too, is open to view on Wednesday afternoons in the summer.

Back at the Visitors' Centre you may have time for a cup of tea before resuming your drive.

Jedburgh has much to offer besides the grandeur of its abbey. This is, probably, the best preserved of all four, despite the numerous occasions on which it was destroyed. The abbey was founded as an Augustine Priory by David I in 1138 but it was not completed until 1227. It is said to have been rebuilt eight times in all but, after particularly severe raids in 1545, further rebuilding was abandoned. The oldest parts to have survived are at the east end and, among its outstanding features are a rose window and its massive transept tower, which rises to 86 feet. The north transept serves as a burial vault for the family of the Marquis of Lothian.

The Jedburgh town centre is full of charm, with the multi-coloured frontages of the buildings and the relaxed and friendly nature of its residents. Tourist buses are much in evidence in summer, spilling out their occupants to disperse to the abbey, the old town jail - now a museum - or to Mary Queen of Scots' House. This sixteenth century town house still shows glimpses of its past as a fortified 'Bastel House', which would have been used by citizens of Jedburgh as a place of refuge during the Border raids. Mary lived there in 1566, when she was only 23 years old and the house is open to visitors as a museum of the period.

Two miles south of Jedburgh off of the A68 stands Ferniehirst Castle. The present castle was built in 1598 to replace an earlier, fifteenth century building. Apart from its many years as a fortress it has served several other purposes. In 1934 it was leased to the Scottish Youth Hostel Association by Philip, the 11th Marquis and continued as a youth hostel until 1985, apart for a period during the Second World War, when it became a barracks for the Royal Artillery Regiment.

Restoration took place during 1984/1987 and the castle was opened to the public in May 1987. Access is only available on Wednesdays during the summer and is limited to two small rooms on the ground floor but it is possible to enjoy an extended tour of the main building by arrangement.

You began your 'pilgrimage' at Berwick on Tweed, on the English side of the border and, as you left Jedburgh to visit Ferniehirst, you would see the sign outside a cafe - 'The last shop in Scotland'. You are on the A68 and, if England is your destination, Newcastle is but a short distance away. If, however, you are remaining in Scotland, the same highway will lead you in the other direction to our capital, Edinburgh. The choice is yours.

Isabel and I hope, if you had not already experienced them, that our photographs will have introduced you to a tiny sample of the beauty of the Borders, an area that so many people - including ourselves until a few years ago - drove through on their way to somewhere else, without realising what they were missing.

Welcome good people. Welcome to my home
(Isabella's Welcome - James Hogg)

Selkirk Municipal Buildings

Jedburgh Town Centre

Borders' Brick & Stone 63

Jedburgh Abbey

Mary Queen of Scots House, Jedburgh

Old Selkirk Brig